From The Heart of The Father
To My Sons and Daughters

By

Tracey De'Andrea Hill

From the Heart of the Father
To My Sons and Daughters
2nd Edition

Contact Information
hilltracey292@gmail.com

Table of Contents

DEDICATION

This book is dedicated to the loving memory of my
grandmother
Florence Elizabeth Hill
and my mother
Doris Evelyn Hill

Thanks
Praise
Glory
Honor

To God and His Son Jesus Christ whom
without nothing is possible

Many see my glory, but few know my story.
What was designed to break me God used it to
make me.
Through my trials I thank You, God, I learned
Your Word and guidance taught me how not to
fear; but to persevere.
You gave me peace amid adversity and assured
me my victory is complete.
Lord, I thank You for being the head of my life.
And in everything I do, I wholeheartedly
acknowledge You!

FORWARD

Inspiring...! Heartfelt...! Touching...! And revealing the very soul of this poet, Tracey De'Andrea Hill. This is a must-read collection of poems by a gifted and talented woman of God.

Tracey, a woman with a quiet nature and humble disposition; openly expresses her true Christian witness of her love for her heavenly Father and her strong conviction of who Jesus Christ is in her life.

Each poem will always point you to her lovingly heavenly Father and her caring Savior Jesus Christ. As you read this work of art, I know that you will be truly blessed, enlightened, and uplifted in these stirring and moving poems of Tracey De'Andrea Hill...Amazing Poems of her heart.

By Dr. Elizabeth Littlefield

ACKNOWLEDGEMENTS

To Apostle Gregory O. Littlefield, my spiritual father, who has spoken words of prophecy into my life on many occasions. Over 10 years ago, at our old church location, when the spirit was high in a Sunday morning church service, God led Apostle Littlefield to call people to the altar to receive any and everything God had for them. I went up to the altar and he took me by my hands and held them high. As he spoke a prophetic word for me, he asked if anyone had ever told me I had million-dollar hands. Indeed no one had; "well you do, and God is going to bless you in the area of writing in ways you cannot imagine." Apostle, I thank you for that word. Ever since that day you prayed for me, I have been writing non-stop.

To Dr. Elizabeth L. Littlefield, my spiritual mother, who has also spoken into my life. I remember being planted as a member of Family of Faith Christian Church. Within a few months of being a member, I was asked to recite one my poems for a Women's Conference: The Threshing Floor of 2006. This was a total surprise for me because I never considered myself to be someone standing before God's people doing anything. Like Apostle Gregory, Dr. Elizabeth Littlefield has also spoken words of encouragement to me in other areas of my life.

Like Apostle Gregory, Dr. Elizabeth Littlefield has also spoken words of encouragement to me in other areas of my life

One Sunday after service she took me by the hand and said, "Tracey, I know you are going to school to learn different things to help you in your professional life but understand that what you are learning how to do will not just be for your professional life only. You will be doing those things and more for the building up of God's kingdom. God is using your pursuit of education to prepare you for your ministry."

Apostle Gregory and Dr. Elizabeth, thank you both not only for praying for me but also for seeing things in me spiritually that I did not see in myself.

To my dear friend Delores Jamison who constantly encourages me to think outside of the box. She convinced me not only to enroll in the Ministry Development Institute at Family of Faith for ministry training, but she also encouraged me to enroll in an accelerated bachelor's program for adults at Texas College.

It was not my plan to go for both degrees at the same time in two years, but since God made the provisions for me to pay for the education, I took advantage of the opportunity. Delores proofread many of my written works, especially when I was pursuing my bachelor's degree. She would keep me up in the wee hours of the morning reading my papers and bloodying them up with red ink showing all the changes I had to make.

I would tell her that I was tired, I did not want her to read any of the papers anymore. I would often say to her go home! "I will go home as soon as you make the changes I have told you to make", she would reply. Doing all that back-to-back studying for two degrees was extremely hard and quite exhausting. Delores helped me to stay focused on the end result which was graduating with honors while receiving both degrees. Delores, I thank you for not giving up on me. And above all, thank you for not allowing me to give up on myself.

To my dear friend, Shelia Williams, who I could truly call anytime, day or night. Thank you for your years of dedicated friendship. You are truly a friend who sticks closer than a brother. You stuck by me during a time when I needed it the most. You not only prayed for me, but when you did not hear from me or could not reach me by phone, you would literally get in your car and drive from Longview to Tyler to see about me. There are not many people in my life who would do that, so I deeply thank you. Shelia, you are a true friend. That is not a statement I can use with everyone.

You are honest with me even though you know the truth may sometimes hurt. Your honesty is done in a way that does not damage me. You tell me the truth in love and that means a lot.

To my dear friend Barbara Luton—not only my first supervisor,—we were co-workers! It was during our work relationship that we became the best of friends.

Barbara, you taught me how to smile through the worst of circumstances. You too are a friend who stuck by me when I needed it the most. You taught me I had the right to make my own choices, even though there were times those choices I made were the wrong ones. As my friend, you respected my right to make my own decisions. Even when I came to myself and realized I was wrong, you did not judge me; like God, you hugged me, loved me, and continued to stand by me.

Barbara, I thank you so much for blessing me during the special times in my life and for those "just because" times as well. Thank you for telling me that I was alright no matter what anybody had to say about me. In our last conversation, you told me how much you loved me and how proud you were of me. You also told me no matter what anyone says about me believe what God says about me. I had the privilege to witness this testimony of your life as you fought a grueling battle with cancer.

No matter what was said or going on you believed what God said and what He would do. That smiling expression showed on your face the day of your homegoing. My dear friend Barbara you are gone but never forgotten. In loving memory.............

To my dear friends Elder Ray and First Lady Diane Beasley, who took me in over 30 years ago when I moved to Tyler. Elder Beasley and First Lady Beasley, you are like brother and sister to me. Their home is always open to me.

Elder Beasley, I thank you for being easy to talk to. You have given me much sound advice over the years, both natural and spiritual. First Lady Diane, you are truly one of a kind. Your generosity has been outstanding. Elder Ray and First Lady Diane, I thank you both for allowing me to be a part of your family and for encouraging me. You understood how hard it was for me to live in a strange place. I did not know anyone, and you willingly embraced me with open arms. I will never forget what the two of you have done for me throughout the years.

To the woman who inspired me to publish my writings, Dr. Sharon Ross, who read some of my writings and asked me the question: Do you want to write so others can profit from your writing, or do you want to write for yourself, and you reap the blessings?

I told her I wanted to write for myself and reap the blessings, but I also want others to profit spiritually and emotionally from the help drawn from page to page. This conversation with her happened over 10 years ago when I was at my lowest.

She told me what to do and gave me a deadline to have my first draft ready. After that I made corrections and as God directed me, I added more and more, and this, has now resulted in the finished product.

Dr. Ross, I thank you for having confidence in my ability to write. I also thank you for your insight in seeing the author in me that I could never imagine seeing in myself. From the bottom of my heart, I thank every one of you for touching my life in a very special way.

PREFACE

We are living in uncertain times that call for hope in God like never before. God desires that all people come to know and love Him the same unconditional way He knows and loves them. Read the poetry and let it be your secret hiding place. In addition to the poetry, during my personal prayer time, God lays it on my heart to chronicle certain things about specific areas of my life I have concerns about. He gives this information to me in the form of letters, and they are as follows:

- It's Time to Be About my Father's Business: This is my testimony about what could have been a near-death experience for me.

- A Single Woman's Marriage Confession: This is about my desire to marry again.

- God's Leading Man: This is encouragement for single men in all walks of life.

Everything written in this book comes not only from the heart of a woman but that of a single woman, a lady in waiting. Although some of the writings pertain to single women, they are also an encouragement to single men who also
desire to marry. There is also encouragement for those single men and women who do not necessarily desire marriage, but they do want to be whole to fulfill their God-given purpose in life and need God's guidance for an abundant life.

I share some of my encounters with God in this book because I learned in life people relate to what they know is real. Sharing my testimony is a way to show what God can and will do in a person's life. It is my prayer this book will highly uplift and encourage all readers to live and be all they can be in God. It is my prayer that everyone who reads and shares the contents of this book be bountifully blessed and experience God in a way they have never experienced Him before.

INTRODUCTION

From the Heart of the Father: To My Sons and Daughters is a book written in its own unique way. Everything written in this book is derived from my quiet times with God. It was during these times God really spoke to my heart about the broken and shattered areas of my life.

The poems were written at a time in my life when I truly had nowhere else to turn but to God. The more time I spent with Him, the more I began to write. Everything in this book reflects me. What I write is an insight of me as a woman, an author a voice for godly expression of peace and freedom. Writing allows me to be transparent. I have learned that through transparency people can relate and respond to what is real. It is through realism that people are encouraged because similar experiences help them understand the process of going through fires and coming out victoriously. If true freedom and peace can happen for Tracey Hill, then it can certainly happen for you!

The other writings mentioned are:

- It's Time to be About My Father's Business
- A Single Woman's Marriage Confession: Daddy's Little Girl
- God's Leading Man

These are what I call letters of encouragement for single men and women. I have a heart for singles, and I have noticed at times we seem to be a forgotten group.

A great deal of prayer and prayer groups focus on the family and relationships. This usually consists of a husband, wife, and children. And most of the time singles are included in this category if they are single parents. Honestly, I do not believe this is an oversight.

I believe most people who are not single, or if they are single and have been with someone for a long time, simply do not think in terms of one. My greatest desire is to encourage single men and women because there is purpose and meaning in our lives. Singles have desires that God is more than happy to fulfill. This book has something for everyone, and my prayer is that it richly blesses everyone who reads it.

CHAPTER ONE

A Tribute To Two Very Special
Women Of My Life
Florence Elizabeth Hill

My grandmother and mother were two very extraordinary women from whom I derived a great deal of inspiration. My grandmother, Florence Hill, worked in a domestic capacity and did not have much formal education. But with her quick wit, wisdom, and uncommon know-how, she was living proof that where there is a will, there is always a way.

Grandma always found a way to accomplish a task whether she had what she needed or not. When I was a child the entire town I lived in experienced a gas shortage. That winter we had no way of cooking anything to eat so we ate bologna sandwiches and potato chips. My grandma said, *"I want a hot meal, and come hell or high water I'm going to have it!"* When we reminded her we did not have gas to cook, she said *"No, but we do have electricity."*

She took an iron, yes, the kind you iron clothes with, placed it in the groove between the stove and kitchen countertop with the flat side up and plugged it in.

She let it get good and hot, put a skillet on top of the iron and put some butter in it.

It took a while to get as hot as she wanted it, but when it was just right, she scrambled fluffy eggs, cooked seasoned bacon, and deliciously grilled buttery toast.

We all looked at her in amazement and she turned and told us *"It's like I always say, where there's a will there's a way."* During the time of the gas shortage, we continued to eat hot meals. Grandma had all kinds of sayings such as, *"Don't take any wooden nickels, if you take them break them. I'm too old of a cat to be called a kitten. Every dog has its day, and every good one has two..."* the list just goes on and on.

Like most grandparents, she told me to keep living, because the older I got the more I would understand, and she was right. She was a woman who you pretty much had to take as she was. Everybody she met was automatically a friend. People were drawn to her because she was real about who and what she was in the community. She always had a way of not only making you laugh, but when you left her presence, you went away with something.

When Grandma died, she did not leave money or land, but she left a legacy that will last a lifetime.

It is a legacy that can be passed down from generation to generation. Grandma taught me that no matter what was going on in my life, to every dark cloud there is a silver lining. Life's happiness is not always about what you do not have, but that which you already possess.

Even when her health had failed her, Grandma still had hope and still had a way of blessing others.

When Grandma blessed others, she felt the act of giving to others was a blessing to her. Sometimes when you think you have it bad, you come across somebody who has it worse. The philosophy she lived by until her dying day was.

> **If I can't help someone in any way, shape, form, or fashion travel this journey called life, then life is truly not worth living. God placed us on earth to be a blessing to each other.**

> **The Late Florence Elizabeth Hill**

Now and Forever an Inspiration to Me

Dear Grandma,

I want to let you know that your life was not in vain. I remember everything you instilled in me growing up as a child into the woman I am now. What you taught me has gotten me through some pretty bleak moments in my life. There were times I found myself asking the question: *What would grandma do in a situation like this?* Since the day I left home and started living on my own, I have used some of those survival techniques you used to do. They really work! You truly showed me that *God can make a way out of no way.*

I remember you telling me:

> **There are things you know how to do
> that no one else can do. There are even
> things you know how to do that you're
> not even aware of.**
>
> **When you come into what God has given
> you, you'll do things and go places you
> never thought you'd go in a million
> years. So, remember I told you that!**
> **The Late Florence Elizabeth Hill**

Once again Grandma you were right, I am doing things and going places I never dreamed possible.

You were a living example of the scripture:

> **Now unto him who is able to do exceedingly
> abundantly above all that we ask or think,
> according to the power that worketh in us.**
> **Ephesians 3:20 KJV**

Thank you, Grandma, for loving and encouraging me. When others said I could not do this, or I did not have what it took to do that...

When others would try to convince you of what I was not capable of, you would tell them *"You don't see in her what I do...not because she's my granddaughter, but because God showed me what she is, what she will be and that's enough for me."* I thank you, Grandma, for mainly seeing in me what I had a hard time seeing in myself and for loving me when I did not love myself.

Grandma, I love you and miss you very much. There is not a day that goes by that I do not wish you were here to ask your advice about something, or to ask you how to do something. But you know what, with all I remember about you, I figured it out and it works. It works because it is what you would do in a situation and what you did always worked. I figure if it worked for you, it would work for me.

Forever in my heart, Tracey.

Doris Evelyn Hill

My mother, Doris Hill, was a high school graduate. She was a straight "A" student, a gifted musician, poet and playwright. She was smart in business and had a way of being there for people even though they were not there for her. She did not get to go to college because she had my brother, myself, and my sister at an early age. She always told us we were the best gift God had given her.

Because of her health, she was not able to work. But she did not let this stop her because she had something going for her, music. She was passionate about the things she loved. She learned to play the piano at an early age and played for the church she grew up in at the age of nine. She played, sang, and wrote songs, plays and poetry. Even though she did not make much money as a church musician, she continued to play anyway because she had a love for it.

Through her music, she was blessed to play, and she sang on live radio and television. She traveled to many places playing and singing for people. When my brother and sister and I were young mama would play and sing to us. She would even teach us how to sing. And with her knowledge of music, all three of us had music lessons.

My brother played piano, trumpet, trombone, baritone, and tuba. I played trombone, baritone, tuba, bass trombone, and the trombone with the F attachment. My sister was a drummer and there was not a drum she could not play. We were all first-chair players and winners of solo and ensemble contests. Since we had a mother who was a musician, we had to practice like nobody's business.

Oh yes, if I did not mention it earlier when I was telling you about my grandma, she played the acoustic guitar. So, as you can see my family has a strong background in music. The poetry on the other hand was a different story. My mother was an inward person; she did not always say what was on her mind or how she felt. She would write what she could not say. It was she who introduced me to poetry. I would read different types of poetry and at first, I did not get it. So, mama would ask me about how my day was at school. I would tell her and then she would say now write that down and I did. Then she showed me how to use different words to describe how I felt, what excited my senses, and how to express it.

In high school English Literature, we learned about the dynamics of poetry. Rhyme and meter, free verse poetry verses rhyming poetry and even haiku were introduced to us. When I learned the dynamics of poetry, it helped me to understand what Mama was teaching me. Mama would write about endless things, from what she was going through, to what she read in a book.

A lady once gave Mama huge boxes of nothing but books about any and everything. My sister and I looked at all those books and said there is no way you can read them all. Mama told us both, watch me. In less than a two-month time span she read every book she was given. The same woman came again and brought her almost the same amount she had brought her before. Every spare moment Mama had she read to herself and to us. My sister and I would go through and read some of the ones she had finished. We then understood why she constantly read because these were books that kept you captivated. They drew you in and made you want to read. If a book piques my interest, then I am captivated.

One of the things that hurt me was after moving several times over the years I was not able to keep up with a lot of Mama's writings, like her plays, songs, and poetry. Just like Grandma, everything my mother instilled in me will last a lifetime. Even though Mama did not get to fulfill a lot of her dreams before she died, she did encourage us to make the most of every opportunity we got to further ourselves.

Everything she knew she taught us before we were school-age, so we were ahead of the game when we started school. Mama struggled to raise my brother and me so she could not afford two sets of school supplies. What she would do was buy one coloring book and one box of crayons.

She would draw the pictures from the coloring book and taught us how to color and draw. She even did letter and number drawings so we could trace them. That is how she taught us to read and write. When our youngest sister came along the set of supplies went to her for school.

Like grandma, mama did what she loved until she was no longer able to do it. Mama also left us a legacy that will last a lifetime. Mama's grandchildren, who she was not blessed to see before she died, inherited some of her passions. My sister's two sons are musically inclined. Her oldest son played guitar, like his great-grandma.

Her youngest son played the tuba, and my brother's daughter does not play any instruments I know of, but I do know she is a songbird. My brother, sister, and I said to each other one time if Mama was alive and still playing the piano she would have her grandchildren at the piano with her like she did with us wherever she would be playing. She would teach them everything she taught us.

Mama, I know you loved me, but you did not always say it.

During most of our time together I did not always know how you felt about me as your daughter or if you were ever proud of me when it came to the things I set out to accomplish. It was only after you died that I was told by a relative how you really felt about me.

A relative of ours told me what your last words were to her. My mother was 33 at the time of this conversation with our relative. She died at the age of 42.

She said, Dee, which is the name this relative called me by, I used to tell your Mama when I died, I wanted her to play and sing a certain song at my funeral. Your Mama told me, you know what, you may outlive me. Your Mama told me there was something she wanted me to do for her.

First, she wanted me to look in on her mother to make sure she was alright. Our relative went on about what Mama asked her to do regarding my brother and sister. Then after she finished, I asked her did Mama ever said anything about me. I asked your mama, well what about Tracey? She said Mama told her I am not worried about Tracey because she is going to be just fine.

She went on to tell my mother, well you know, as a child Tracey was considered slow (mentally retarded). My Mama told her I know, but you do not know Tracey like I do. There is more to her than the limitations everybody in the family and outside has tried to put on her. I know my Tracey and I know she will succeed in any and everything she sets out to do in life.

You too are Now and Forever an Inspiration to Me.

Dear Mama,

I want you to know I remember those unspoken moments in my life when you expressed how proud you were of me and how deeply you loved me. During the times I was in the marching band in high school, the band director gave me a trombone solo to play before the crowd for the halftime show. You were scheduled to work the concession stand with some of the other band parents and you were not able to see me perform, or so I thought. The band director told me as I got ready to perform my mama was right there beside him. He said to Mama I thought you had to work the concession stand tonight. She said I do, but I got someone to work for me just long enough for me to see my baby perform before the masses. This is a parent's dream to see their child perform and I will move heaven and earth to see this moment.

I also remember the time you spent making my first dress for my eighth-grade prom. You had one of my aunts spend a whole day with me working on my hair and makeup for that special night. When my makeover was completed, you said, look at my raven beauty. Mama, I thank you for showing me how much you love me in the way you knew how. I also thank you for having unshakable confidence in me and seeing me as the godly beauty I had a hard time seeing myself as.

I was blessed to keep two of the poems you wrote, and I had them put in this book so one of your passions can be shared with the world. Mama, having your poetry in print is my gift to you. I want others to take a glimpse into some of your innermost thoughts on things concerning life as well as what God gave you to write about His love and the relationship he longs to have with His people.

The two poems of yours I am putting in this book tell me just how you really felt about me. They tell me that you truly loved me as God does unconditionally, and you were a friend to me the way no one else has or ever will be. Like grandma, you saw in me what I did not see in myself. I thank you for not only believing, but without a shadow of a doubt knowing, I could and will succeed. Thank you for leaving me a legacy like no other.

Mama, one of your dreams has come true. Your poetry will be read all around the world. Like you mama, there are times in my life when what I cannot say in words has to be expressed in writing. Thank you for developing me in written expression.

Passionately printing, Tracey

CHAPTER TWO

A POEM OF TRIBUTE TO
MY GRANDMOTHER AND MOTHER

There's not a day that goes by
I don't think about you
Whatsoever things are true...honest, just, pure, lovely... think on these
things

Philippians 4:8 KJV

I MISS YOU

You've been an inspiration to me since I was a little girl,
to the woman I am today.
Your love for me was unwavering.
I miss you.
You continued to embrace me as well as correct me
when I needed it.
You left me an inheritance that's more than all the
money in the world.
I miss you.
Grandma, mama: you're both loved and missed.
For everything God blessed you to be for me,
thank you.
You're forever on my mind as well as in my heart.
The end of your life was the beginning of my start.
And yes, I miss you.

CHAPTER THREE

**POETRY WRITTEN BY
THE LATE DORIS EVELYN HILL
LOVE UNCONDITIONAL**

Love me without fear

Trust me without questioning

Need me without demanding

Want me without restriction

Accept me without change

Desire me without inhibitions

For a love so free will never fly away

A FRIEND

A friend is...

Someone who you can share your inner feelings with,

knowing you won't be judged or rejected.

Someone who gives freely without expectation or motivation.

Someone who lets you be who you are.

If you want to change, it's up to you.

Someone who is there when you are hurting—offering their tenderness.

Someone who gives you space when it's needed without hesitation.

Someone who listens to what you're really saying.

Someone who will consider your different beliefs without judgment.

Someone who you always feel close to,

even when they're far away.

Someone who is comfortable to be with—anytime, anywhere, doing anything.

A friend is a special gift to be cherished forever.

26

CHAPTER FOUR

POETRY BY TRACEY D. HILL
God longs for you to know who He is.
So each day take time to be still.
because He is God

HE IS GOD

As we live this life there are many different phases we go through.
When we are at our happiest, things are going so well that
the blessings of God seem to be overtaking us,
remember He is God.
When we are at our saddest, things are happening to us at a
rate so fast that we don't know if the pain will ever end,
remember He is God.
When we get so angry and frustrated at life's outcomes,
more so when we know we've done all we know to do in God's sight,
remember He is God.
God made us a promise that he will be with us always,
even until the end of the earth.
And with that thought in mind,
remember He is God!

You are God's image personified.
You embody everything He is
So know who and what God says you are
YOU ARE

You are gifted because I've given you gifts I've given no other.

You are brilliant because I've given you a mind I've given no other.

You are beautiful because I've given you a beauty I've given no other.

You are unique because I've created you like I've created no other.

You are kind because I've given you a heart only I can give.

You are loving because I've given you a love only I can give.

God created us in His image and everything He created He says is good.

He also says we're fearfully and wonderfully made.

He is everything, and so are you. He created you that way.

Never forget who and what God says you are!

God is a God of impossibilities. He takes the many impossibilities and creates possibilities.

And because you can do all things through Him there's nothing you can't achieve. This is true because God said so.

BECAUSE GOD SAID SO

Man says your limitations make it impossible for you to do the job at hand.

Somehow, despite your limitations, you're blessed to do the job anyway.

Why?

Because God said so.

Man says you can't own your dream house.

Somehow, despite the impossibility, you're blessed with the house anyway.

Why?

Because God said so.

Man sees your limitations as impossibilities.

God sees them as opportunities to work in your life.

God says you can do all things through His son Christ who gives you strength.

He also says He's the author and finisher of your faith.

So no matter what limitations man tries to put on you,

God has the last say so about your life.

So remember when man says no you can't, you just say yes I can.

Why?

Because God said so!

Life is a day-by-day process. From the smallest to the greatest of needs there's nothing God won't provide for you. So instead of pondering on what to do just take it day by day.

Therefore, I say unto you, take no thought for your life, what ye shall eat, or what ye shall drink; nor yet for your body, what ye shall put on. Is not life more than meat, and the body than raiment?

Behold the fowls of the air; for they sow not, neither do they reap, nor gather into barns; yet your heavenly Father feedeth them. Are ye not much better than they?

Matthew 6:25-26 KJV

DAY BY DAY

Lord, when I didn't know where I would live,

You blessed me with shelter for the day.

Lord, I thank You, but this is only for today.

What will I do after this day? Please Lord, what do You say?

Don't worry my child, just take it day by day.

Lord, when I didn't know what I was going to eat,

You blessed me with food for the day.

Lord, I thank You, but this is only for today.

What will I do after this day? Please Lord, what do You say?

Don't worry my child, just take it day by day.

The Lord tells us not to worry, He even says, "don't fret."

He said He would supply all our needs and He's never failed us yet.

We shouldn't worry about tomorrow.

We shouldn't worry about trouble.

He erases all the sorrow, and our blessing He will double.

So when you wonder what you will do after today,

God will remind you:

Don't worry my child,

Just take it day by day!

God will take the simplest of things you give Him as an act of love and worship. He gets the greatest joy out of them. The best gift you can give Him is you.

GIVE ME YOU

Lord, how I long to sing a song about Your love,

But I don't have the voice it takes to sing of Your glory.

Oh Lord, what can I possibly give You?

The Lord says, give me you.

Lord, how I long to tell people about Your goodness,

But I don't have the etiquette of speech it takes to speak of Your glory.

Oh Lord, what can I possibly give You?

The Lord says, give me you.

Lord, how I long to write so others can read about Your greatness,

But I don't have the skill it takes to write of Your glory.

Oh Lord, what can I possibly give?

The Lord says, give me you.

When we look at everything God is, we pale in comparison.

When God sees we have a heart to want to live for Him, it fills His heart with gladness.

And it gives Him joy unspeakable.

God loves us so much that all He wants is us, imperfections and all.

He will take everything we're not and make us into everything He created us to be.

So when you ask the Lord, "What can I possibly give You?"

The Lord will lovingly say, give me you!

Life is not a matter of what you possess. Life is a matter of who you trust.

Trust in the Lord with all thine heart; and lean not to thine own understanding. In all thy was acknowledge Him, and He shall direct thy paths.

Proverbs 3:5-6 KJV

IT'S A MATTER OF TRUST

In life, we place our trust in a lot of things.

Some of us have riches beyond our wildest dreams,

so much so that we don't know what to do with them.

Some of us have beauty that's beyond compare,

so much so that it will make a man or woman's heart skip a beat.

Some of us have so much success and popularity

that we can't be in two or three places at one time.

It's not a sin in God's sight that we have all of this.

After all, it's because of Him we are blessed in these areas of our lives.

However, in having all this one truth remains,

it's a matter of trust.

The word of God says we should trust the Lord

with all our heart, mind, soul, our everything.

God in His infinite wisdom and love

put this fact in His word

because He knows these things are not everlasting.

It's easy to trust God

when we have all these things working in our favor.

However, the inevitable comes into play:

Riches can be lost or stolen, and beauty fades;

success and popularity eventually die.

When all these things are no longer working for us,

one truth remains:

it's a matter of trust.

People respond to what is real. When others encounter you and see
Christ-like characteristics, you're living a life that's genuine and true.

A LIFE GENUINE AND TRUE

Let this mine which is in Christ be in you
Let His word abide in you and be true
For it's the perfecting of your faith
When you learn not only to trust but also wait
Oh Lord because I live a life of service to You
Let everything I do be genuine and true
When you run this life's race
Stay focused, not on speed, but a slow and steady pace
When running this race don't worry about how long it takes
For God only requires you to finish strong for your sake
For if you truly endure until the end
Without a shadow of a doubt you will surely win
After you've withstood every attack Satan devised
God will joyfully award you the ultimate prize
Remember as you go through life's hard trials
God promises that living for Him is worthwhile
As you purpose in your heart to abide in God's word
And allow His word to abide in you
Your life of service to Him will then be genuine and true

You are one of a kind, created with beauty and strength. This is what makes you a woman of destiny

WOMAN OF DESTINY

Woman of destiny, here you stand, made with pride and virtue that's true
There's nothing My hands have made that compares to the beauty of you
You are truly a purpose by design
For when I made you I had destiny in mind
I edified you to go North, South, East and West
To draw men and women for the upbuilding of
My kingdom so the world can see My glory at its best
I have for you living examples of women from the days of old
In the bible, their stories are told
Like Deborah, a prophet, songwriter, counselor and mother
A true warrior for Me like no other
Like Esther, who won the heart of a king with a beauty enhanced with humility and grace
Who willingly risked life itself to save the Jewish race
Like the virtuous woman who used My wisdom to live life at its best
When people encountered her they were truly blessed
Like Mary who humbly submitted to My will enduring its high price
She gave birth to your Lord and Savior Jesus Christ
Like all women you have experienced some hurts you could have allowed your hearts to foster
But you know My word says no weapon that's formed against you shall prosper
In the same way you can learn from these women of old you can learn from each other
Young women learn from the old as if they were their mothers
Women of destiny be beautiful, bold, proud, and true
For there is truly no one like you

Even in the darkest of times when God's presence isn't felt, He has a way of telling you I'm here.

I'M HERE

Twenty-three years ago, during that special moment in your life.

When you gave birth to your daughter, both our eyes filled with joyful tears

Yes my daughter, I'm here

As she grew up and got through those triumphant as well as trying years

Yes my daughter, I'm here

And now at the most devastating moment of your life.

The loss of a child we both hold so near and dear

Yes my daughter, I'm here

As your heart aches and breaks, as you cry endless tears

Yes my daughter, I'm here

In every moment of your life, from the happiest to the saddest,

I've been with you

Just as I rejoiced with you, I now mourn with you

As you cry, I hold you and cry as well. I tell you this because

I made a promise to you

I'll never leave nor forsake you

My daughter always know

no matter what you go through in life

Never forget, I'm here

Through every season in life take time to reflect on God's goodness in the midst of them.

A TIME OF REFLECTION

A time to laugh

A time to cry

A time to rejoice

A time to mourn

A time to speak

A time to be silent

A time to pray

A time to stand still

A time to forget

A time to reflect

In life there's a time and a season for everything

There's a time for us to live for the moment and move on the things of God without delay

There's also a time for us to reflect on past mistakes, hurts, troubles, trials and triumphs

When we reflect it's to help us remember God's hand in our lives through its various stages

When we reflect on His goodness through all of this it helps us to understand who He is so remember God in a time of reflection.

My patience is enduring and My love is everlasting. No matter what you've done or how long you've been gone. You can always come back to Me.

COME BACK TO ME

Seek me while I may be found

So you will be free and not be bound

Oh how I await you with open arms

For it's My heart's desire to protect you from all harm

My child, My child come back to Me

For only I can truly set you free
I am the peace to life's many storms
As I continue to await you with open arms
Just call on the name of Jesus and see
Satan has no choice but to flee
My child, My child come back to me
For only I can truly set you free
You can search the world for all eternity
But your answers you will find only in Me
Satan only wants to blind you to your fear
But you forget I'm a God who's always near
My child, My child come back to Me
For only I can truly set you free
Oh how I love you don't you see
For I sent My son Jesus to die just for thee
Father I walked away I'm too far from thee
How can you possibly continue to love and stay with me
Because I made a promise to be with you through all eternity
So again I say My child, My child come back to Me
For only I can truly set you free!
Your oneness is in Me

THIS I VOW

I will take you as my husband to be
I will love, honor and cherish thee
To you I will respect and be true
Even in the midst of whatever I go through
My parents I leave to you I cleave
Because you're the love of my heart
Only in death will we part
Whoever tries to separate us I won't allow
Before God this day I vow
I will take you as my wife

I will love, honor and cherish you for life
To provide for, protect and be true
Even in the midst of whatever we go through
My parents I leave to you I cleave
Because you're the love of my heart
Only in death will we part
Whoever tries to separate us I won't allow
Before God this day I vow
Husband and wife I hear what you say
And I the Lord Your God promise you on this day
If you truly trust and believe
Ask anything according to My will and you'll receive
Before Me this day you've become one
No man shall separate you because in Me victory's won
I promise to be with you
Even in the midst of whatever you go through
If you keep Me the center of your life I'll take away all misery and strife
Because to Me your lives you freely give
You shall not die but truly live
No hurt or harm to your marriage will I allow
Before you this day from the Lord Your God I Vow

Before you this day from the Lord Your God I vow!
My life is incomplete without you my lover and my friend

MY LOVER AND MY FRIEND

My wife is a woman who's beautiful, kind, compassionate and true
There's no greater gift I've ever received that compares to you
For God with His wisdom and love from above
Gave me a woman with whom I'm crazy in love
A woman who promises to love and stick by me to the end
My wife, my lover and my friend
My husband, a man who's handsome, bold, loving and strong

I thank God for the gift of patience because I waited so long
For God with His abundant love for me
Gave me a man who I can truly love and be free
A man who promises to love and stick by me to the end
My husband, my lover and my friend
Husband and wife you are no longer two but one
Everything you have is no longer yours or mine, for ours is
what it has become
Some phases of marriage take some getting used to
But once you get used to seeing your new life from this perspective,
you'll learn what to do
When you commit yourselves to one another you no longer want to be
alone
Because it's when you're together you both stand strong
The same commitment you made to Me you made to each other
So forever remain each other's friend and lover.

My Son and the cross are the depth of My love for you.
I LOVE YOU MORE THAN I CAN SAY

Since before the foundation of the world you have been on My mind
Before your parents got together, you were conceived not knowing
if you were going to be a boy or a girl
The day you opened your eyes, took your first breath of life,
and cried announcing your arrival into the world, I knew you
Throughout your life as you grew. During the good and bad times,
the times you made Me laugh as well as cry
During the times you strayed, chose not to listen to Me and not do what
I say.
When you said and did things that hurt Me like you wouldn't believe
Through all of that I love you more than I can say
I already knew what was going to happen beforehand. That's why I gave
the ultimate sacrifice, My son Jesus Christ. He took on the devastation of
being temporarily separated from Me, a fate worse than death itself
All because I love you more than I can say
Because of Jesus' death, you're once again in right standing with Him.
You've finally longed for the best gift anyone can have and that's a
relationship with Me
You've learned to walk and talk with Me again. You share your secrets
and I share Mine
We have a love affair that's beyond the imagination. A day never goes by
that you don't think of Me and I you
As you past the tests of life, cross the finish line and receive the winner's
cup, we celebrate victory at last and have a royal feast that never ends
As we embrace one another and make our eternal connection speaking
in the same breath I love you more than I can say

God wants you to know He is the I am of your life.

I AM YOUR PEACE

I am the calm to your storm

I am the quietness to your chaos

I am the serenity and tranquility

To all that disturbs you

I am your peace

Never sell yourself short because God sees great value in you

NEVER

Never stop praying

Never stop hoping

Never stop dreaming

Never stop believing

Never stop achieving

Never stop doing your best

Never say you can't go to college because you're not smart enough

Never say you can't get a husband because men don't think you're pretty

Never believe a negative report about yourself from anyone including you

What man says you can't do God says you can

Never give up because there are no limits to God

He is absolute and He never makes a promise He won't keep

So never say never

Like the eagle you can rise above any situation

THE EAGLE

Like the eagle you are majestic

Like the eagle you soar high

Like the eagle you sometimes must fly away to the highest mountain to get away from the masses

It is there you tear your old feathers, sharpen your beak, and purify yourself in the eternal waterfalls of nature

Like the eagle, after its grueling process of restoration, you come out anew

Like the eagle you soar higher than before

Like the eagle you rise above adversity

Like the eagle you are strong and steadfast

Like the eagle you are rare because there are not many like you

My child take heart because what I placed in the eagle, I placed in you

Like the eagle you are majestic, beautiful and strong

You can rise above any of life's challenges

Therefore, My child, in everything trust Me and have patience

Because the only direction I have for you is an upward one

So mount up on your wings and take flight, just like the eagle

When God asked Solomon what he wanted, Solomon asked for
wisdom so he could better rule God's people.
Since Solomon did not ask for riches, God gave him wisdom as well as
riches
Wisdom is the principal thing, therefore get wisdom; and with all thy
getting get understanding

Proverbs 4:7 KJV

WISDOM

Wisdom surpasses intelligence, skill, beauty and brawn
Wisdom unlocks the door to endless possibilities
Wisdom is the key to fulfilling the divine purpose God has for
you
Wisdom is the best gift God can give
May the wisdom of God follow for the rest of your life

Whoso findeth a wife findeth a good thing,
and obtaineth favor of the Lord

Proverbs 18:22 KJV

THE FIRST

To your first

Promise
Kiss
Dance
Year
Anniversary
Child/Children

When a man finds a wife, he finds a good thing and obtains favor from
the Lord
God has blessed the two of you to find each other and He knew before
you both knew you would become one

This is to all the first in your new life together. May God richly bless the two of you in your new life together

CHAPTER FIVE

A MESSAGE FROM THE LORD
Thursday, July 11, 2013
8:31 PM

A Message from the Lord

Dear Tracey:

RE: It's Time to Be About My Father's Business

Tracey, it's been a very long time since I've talked to you in this manner. I'm glad you and I are talking again I've really missed you. This has been a really trying year for you in the area of your health. Seven years ago, Satan attacked your health to the point the doctors were afraid if they sent you home you wouldn't live to see the next day. Barely able to talk with shallow breath you begged and pleaded with them not to admit you into the hospital back then.

Against their better judgment, they didn't admit you, but they kept you there and kept a close watch over you. You were nervous and scared and they realized that was making things worse. So, while the doctor got you in a calm state the nurse gave you a shot in your IV so you could breathe easily and rest. After you became stabilized the doctors did release you but not before they held you longer to make sure the meds fully freed your lungs to breathe before you could go home.

As the nurse was releasing you, she asked why you didn't call someone for help, and how did you get to the state you took the risk of driving yourself to the hospital. I don't even know how you could have even gotten yourself up, let alone get in a car and drive.

Tracey, you told the nurse it wasn't that I WOULDN'T call someone. I PHYSICALLY COULDN'T call anyone. Since I couldn't physically call on a person, I called on the Lord and when you call on Him, He will answer, that's how I got to the hospital.

Tracey, after you walked out of the hospital that day you have no idea how what you said to that nurse impacted her life. Your testimony all those years ago made a real difference for her. After that episode Tracey you got started on the road to good health for yourself. You got under personal trainers, watched what you ate, and managed and maintained a healthy weight loss for over five years.

As time went on in the process of your newfound health you started working on your higher educational goals to embark on a new career path. When this took place in your life it brought on new health challenges you never imagined. These health challenges didn't come about because of not eating and doing all the right things. You tried to do some things with your own strength. You were under so much stress and pressure to accomplish goals for yourself that the result could have been catastrophic.

Monday, April 14, 2013, at 7:00 AM you were almost dressed and ready to start your busy day. As a woman, you're a multi-tasker and your mind was so consumed with everything you had to do just for the day. You didn't miss a beat and as you were about to put the rest of our clothes on and start your day, you were stopped dead in your tracks.

On that unforgettable day Tracey, in the physical you were all alone, but in the spirit, Me (God) My son (Jesus), and the Holy Spirit were right there with you the whole time.

When you were asked what happened you really couldn't tell anyone because there was not a physical witness. Tracey because I'm a God who promises to never leave or forsake you, you had Me. Tracey, you had a seizure that almost caused you to have a stroke. All of this was brought on by stress and being overworked. You were doing so much you didn't even feel the warning signs letting you know you needed to slow down.

You had no control over your body, you couldn't speak, move, or scream out for help.

In the physical you were unconscious, but your spirit man was well alert and that's when I, My Son, and the Holy Spirit ministered to you. I didn't come in a thunderous manner, but I came in a still small voice and brought these two things back to your remembrance:

I will keep him in perfect peace whose mind is stayed on thee

Philippians 3:10 KJV

When you call on the name of the Lord I will answer

Psalms 91:15 KJV

Tracey when I blessed you to remember how I brought you out from your first brush with death experience you regained consciousness saying **LORD I NEED YOU!!!** Tracey, you never told anyone about the first brush with death you had, not even your brother and sister. I have you tell this now because my single sons and daughters need to be encouraged by your testimony.

There are many single men and women who, just like you, are physically alone. Yes, Tracey I'm with you, I'm with everyone, but the reality is physically you're alone, and in situations like the one you've experienced it's terrifying.

Tracey, I have you to write about your life-changing experience to help encourage those single men and women who are alone physically. Some of these men and women are single parents who have not just themselves but their children to consider. People who are husband and wife, theoretically, are each other's backup. The single man or women, with or without children, don't have that backup. And if they go down there's physically no one there to help pick up the slack.

Tracey that's why I have you title this message ***It's Time to Be About My Father's Business***. And now that I have your undivided attention, you've procrastinated long enough. It's truly time for you to be about My (God's) business.

· This book

· The ministry you've submitted to your pastors to reach a people of a different culture

· Singles

Tracey, many of my single sons and daughters don't have an inkling of the purpose and destiny I have in store for them. I have the answers and the help they need; they just need a living example to help guide them to it. Tracey singles need to see, with My help, they can accomplish great things. I can minimize their stress; I can increase their finances so they can better provide and leave an inheritance for their children.
I can bless them with that mate they desire while they are waiting. With My help they too can be about their father's business.
My single sons and daughters need help knowing and understanding that if they:

**Seek ye first the kingdom of God
and all His righteousness, all
these things will be added unto you
Matthew 6:33 KJV**

**Delight thyself also in the Lord
and he shall give thee the desires
of thine heart.**

Psalms 37:4 KJV

Tracey, the above-mentioned goes to you as well. I know you have plans and goals for your life and that's a good thing. This time I want you to wholeheartedly commit your plans to Me. Not only do I want you to commit them to Me, I want you to abandon them altogether.

> **For I know the plans I have for you,**
> **declares the Lord. Plans to prosper**
> **you and not to harm you plans**
> **to give you hope and a future.**

Jeremiah 29:11 KJV

Tracey, no one knows half of what I've brought you through. This book is true life and there are not many of them out there, especially when it comes to reaching people who are single just like you.

Tracey, I have you to write this book because My people as a whole need to know I talk to them, I listen to them, I'm concerned about them, and I love them. For over seven years Tracey I've communicated to you through writing, the same way I did through your mother when she was alive. I did it with her through poetry and music. I do it through you with poetry, music, sign language and personal letters.

This isn't the first time I've communicated to you this way and it won't be the last. This isn't a letter of chastisement it's a letter telling you I'm with you and I deeply love you. My hand of protection is all over you and I want to do the same for all singles.

Tracey, Sunday, June 30, 2013, during a morning service no message was taught. The Spirit of Praise was so high that everyone who was open received what they needed and more. Your pastor called all ministers to the alter and gave each and every one a charge from Me (God) to be about My business.

Tracey you've been given more than a second chance and I know you know that you've walked with Me for far too long not to know who and what I am in your life. Tracey My personal charge to you is to have this book finished and published.

Tracey when this book is read, and it transforms the hearts and minds of those who read it. They will see ***"From the Heart of the Father: To My Sons and Daughters"*** is more than just a title.

Tracey now like never before it is time to BE ABOUT YOUR FATHER'S BUSINESS!!!

Know that I love you and all that's yours.

With Love

From the Lord Your God

CHAPTER SIX

WORDS OF ENCOURAGEMENT FOR SINGLE MEN AND WOMEN
A MESSAGE FROM THE LORD
Sunday, March 21, 2010
5:40 AM

A Message from the Lord

Dear Tracey:

RE: A Single Woman's Marriage Confession

God's desire is for you to maintain a relationship with Him. When you do this everything in your life will fall into place

Tracey D. Hill

I know your heart desires to marry. Marriage is a good thing because I created it. It is not a wrong desire to have at all. But what I require from you right now is to open yourself up to the idea of a courtship with Me. Yes, Tracey, I want to woo you, I want to cherish you. I want the two of us to have an intimacy that's beyond your wildest imagination. When a truly intimate relationship happens between us, nothing can break it because we're together. It will be the same way with who I already have in mind for you to marry.

Tracey, do you know why I stress the importance of maintaining a relationship with Me?

This is because in times past a man had to get permission from the father of the woman, he was interested in just to even talk to her. A woman's father is a watcher and keeper. A man knows the mentality of another man and a father has the wisdom to know whether a man will truly take care of his daughter the way he should.

A true father will not willingly give his daughter away to a man who will abuse her. That's why the father insists on meeting any man who has an interest in her because a true father wants what's best for his daughter.

Tracey, your father missed out on a golden opportunity to be a part of your life. When a natural father is absent from a woman's life she is left to the wolves. Your grandmother and mother did all they knew how to do with the knowledge they had.

However, without any positive male role model in a woman's life to help her understand the type of men she should stay away from, she's pretty much left to fend for herself and must learn some things about men the hard way. And some of these things, without My intervention, can take a woman to a point of no return.

Tracey, you've gone through a lot in the area of men. I've constantly watched over you and I continued to remain a constant in your life, even when you walked away from Me years after you divorced your husband because of the continual hurt. You were so hurt to the point that you didn't trust anyone, including Me.

Even during the time you walked away and left My protection I still covered you and will forever cover you.

Tracey, I do this because you're My daughter and I have a love for you that's beyond compare to anything a man on earth can have for you.

As your Heavenly Father it's My responsibility to watch over and protect you because you're My little girl. Yes, Tracey, I know you're a grown woman, but in the eyes of every father no matter how old his daughter is, she will always be seen as his little girl.

Men for the past few years have passed you up as if you didn't exist. I know this deeply hurts you and it makes you feel like there's something wrong with you. Tracey, it's not you, I'm intervening in this area of your life because my little girl deserves the best there is. Tracey that's where the intimate relationship with Me comes in. Continue to stay open to My direction in all the areas of your life. Because Tracey it's My guidance you follow to help you avoid pitfalls and hurts.

The man I have for you cannot only wear the title "Head" but can handle the responsibility that comes along with being the "Head". He will be able to talk to another woman and still only have eyes for you. He's not insecure and will trust your ability to talk to another man and you stay faithful to him. Tracey what I have for you is for you. No matter how much another person tries to block things, when I orchestrate the time and opportunity for the two of you to get acquainted nothing can stop it.

So Tracey, continue to be who I made you to be, beautiful and confident in who you are. You don't have to make things happen with a man and you don't have to lower your standards and openly make it known to others who are present that the two of you are together.

You don't have to work for and pursue the man, he must work for and pursue you because you're the prize.

So Tracey just be yourself because there are men who are taking notice of you in secret. My glory is on your life, and it shows that these men who secretly admire you from far off have such respect for the Christ in you that they will not approach you out of fear of disrespecting you. This is because a man knows when he's in the presence of a true lady.

But when this man does have the boldness to approach and he approaches you in the right way, you'll know what to do. Tracey, know I love you and I'm watching over you, and know that I'm your heavenly father. I love you and have nothing but the best for you. Stay encouraged and keep doing what you're doing.

With love

From the Lord Your God!

A MESSAGE FROM THE LORD
Saturday, July 24, 2010
7:30 AM

A Message from the Lord

My Sons:

RE: God's Leading Man

My sons, I want you to know I hear your words and I know what's in your hearts. I know some of you desire wives just like my daughters desire husbands. Most women feel like men are only after one thing. They feel like men only want to love them and leave them and unfortunately in some cases that has been true. Because of the actions of some men, it has made it hard for the truly good men to make any progress with women.

My sons I know that all men are not the user/abuser or the love them and leave them type. Just like women have been hurt by men some men have been hurt by women. And sometimes a man's hurt can go far deeper than that of a woman. This is because as little boys men were taught to be tough, real men don't cry. If they are hurt they don't show it.

My sons, all of the misconceptions you've been taught are lies. I created you not only to be the provider and protector; I also created you to be passionate, caring, tender and loving. In the same way men want a woman whom they feel is highly attractive physically, women want a tall dark and handsome man. It's easy for men and women to get caught up in the superficial.

In the same way women don't want to be rejected by men because they sometimes feel a man would never give them the time of day because they're not considered beautiful, this applies to men who think women won't go for them because they're not considered handsome.

Men listen up. There is a man in the bible who dispelled all the myths.

He hath no form of comeliness.
and when we shall see Him, there is
no beauty that we should desire Him.

Isaiah 53:2 KJV

My sons, I hear you say that the man I'm describing doesn't exist. I'm here to tell you that he does.

This man embodied everything I mentioned earlier to you and more. Even though he was not the most handsome man on the earth, women swooned over him like you would not believe.

This man embodied love and compassion when it came to women that He awakened such an arousal in them that it surpassed any sexual experience a woman could ever have. One woman worshiped and adored Him so she kneeled in reverence of his lordship by washing his feet with her tears and dried them with her hair.

One woman He approached; He spoke to her heart in such a way that He didn't define her by her past.

Instead, He gave her living water and she became a witness for him telling others about what an amazing man she met.

Another woman He encountered was considered the sinner of all sinners, but instead of casting the first stone He picked her up from a fallen state, forgave her sins and she began life anew.

Another woman who spent all she had on doctors to get well. When she got news of His arrival, she was so drawn by His love and compassion based solely on what she heard that by touching the hem of His garment, her faith brought her complete healing.

This man has so much love and passion for women they not only would, but they did follow Him until the day He died. This man who was and is still the captivator of women's hearts wants to be the captivator of your hearts my sons. My sons this man's name is Jesus and he's the example I sent to earth not only for my daughters but also for my sons to live by. Jesus is a leading man and so are you.

My sons Jesus was born to help you rethink your position in life. Again, just like women have been hurt and devastated by men, men have gone through the same thing with women. And again, in some cases, on a deeper level.

My sons I'm a God who reveals wonders and mysteries and I want to reveal them to you. Those of you who truly desire the love of your life can have her and more. Do you know that the best way to get to know a woman is to get to know her father?

Well, my sons, when you and I get to know one another, you will get to know and find the woman I have designed especially for you.

My sons intimacy begins with Me and when the two of us get to know one another I will reveal the woman who I made just for you.

**Whoso findeth a wife findeth
a good thing, and obtaineth favor
of the Lord.**

Proverbs 18:22 KJV

Men, just like the woman with the issue of blood who tried everything, so have you. But the only thing you haven't tried is Me. I'm your father, I know what's best, and what I will do for my daughters I will do for my sons. Like some of my daughters, some of my sons grew up without a positive male role model, or worse grew up with a model who was cruel, abusive and heartless to you and your mother and this distorted your view on who and what a real man should be.

In most cases a mother is the most stable person a man can have in his life. Sons, even though your natural fathers may have been absent from your life, I, your heavenly father, was and I am still there. You men who are blessed to have your mothers in your life, be open to the wisdom I gave her when it comes to the type of woman you choose to marry.

The same way a man knows the mentality and motives of another man, a woman knows the mentality and motives of another woman.

A mother will know by meeting and spending time with the woman if she will stand by you when things are going bad just as she would when things are going well.

A mother will know if this woman loves and cares for a man for who and what he is, and if she only wants him for what he has and has no desire for him whatsoever. The same way a mother can pick up on the bad qualities in a woman, she can pick up the good qualities in her. A mother will love you as her son and let you know, hey son, you have a good woman here, and if her son isn't doing right by the woman, the mother will let him know he's throwing away his blessing. Sons, your mothers want the same thing I want for you, and that's the best.

That's why this woman called ***MOTHER*** has this special role in your life. My sons, the same way I love my single daughters I love my single sons. I sincerely love every one of you and all that's yours. Take heart and know that I, your Heavenly Father, have everything you need. And when you and I grow in our relationship together I will ignite the love and passion I placed in you in such a way, for the men who desire wives, when you find the woman I have for you, you'll know the right thing to say and do. She will know you truly love her, and it won't be hard for her to submit to you as her cover.

For my sons who don't desire marriage but desire to have fulfillment in life. If you follow my guidance for your life, I will bless you to be a blessing to everyone you meet, and not just financially, this will include influence.

So, to my leading men take heart and be encouraged. And know whatever your heart's desire I'm more than able to fulfill them. The is nothing I will keep from you that will benefit you.

> **For I know the plans I have for you, declares the Lord.**
> **Plans to prosper you and not to harm you, plans to give**
> **you**
> **hope and a future.**

Jeremiah 29:11 KJV

Trust Me (God) to bless you where you are as you surrender the plans for your life to me. I will flourish you and before you know it the desires of our heart will manifest in natural in astonishing ways.

Remember I love you and all that's yours.

With love,
From the Lord your God!

CONCLUSION

To Daddy's Little Girls and God's Leading Men: make the Lord the delight of your lives.

**Delight thyself also in the Lord
and he shall give thee the desires
of thine heart.**

Psalms 37:4 KJV

It is when you take delight in the things of God that pleases Him and in turn He delights in you.

My single men and women intimacy starts with God and when an intimate relationship begins with Him, He will awaken passions in you that no man or woman will be able to resist. The same way it worked for Jesus it will work for you. God wants you to live a fulfilled life both naturally and spiritually. If you truly allow Him to direct you in all areas of your life, He will make all things possible for you.

I do understand it is not every single man and woman's desire to marry and that is also good. There can be contentment in remaining single.

Two examples of a single man and woman who lived fulfilled lives for the Lord are Dorcas (Acts 9:36-42) and Paul (Acts 7:58-28:31) through the New Testament.

Dorcas was a woman who used her gift of sewing by making coats and different garments for the poor. Paul was a man who had such a zeal for serving God he is known in the bible as the world's greatest missionary.

The same way God has examples of good solid men and women who were successful in marriage and family, you now know about a single man and woman who remained content in their single state.

**for I have learned, in whatsoever
state I am, therewith to be ye content.**

Philippians 4:11 KJV

My single men and women know that God has everything you need for your life. Make Him the center of everything and watch what He does for you.

There is a blessing in waiting on God and His time for all things in your lives. Be encouraged and know that God loves you and I do too.

With Love from Your Single Sister in Christ

Love Unconditional
Jeremiah 31:3, 1 John 4:8-12
A Friend
John 15:13
He is God
Psalms 86:1-7
You Are
Genesis 1:26-31, Psalms 139:14
Because God Said So
Philippians 4:13
Day by Day
Matthew 6:25-26, Matthew 34
Give Me You
Judges 3:15-30, Matthew 14:19-22, Acts 9:36-42
It's A Matter of Trust
Proverbs 3:5
Woman of Destiny
Genesis 2:18-23, Judges 4-5, Luke 1:2-28
A Life Genuine and True
Philippians 2:5
I'm Here
Genesis 50:1-11
A Time of Reflection
Ecclesiastes 3:1
Come Back to Me
James 5:19-20
This I Vow
Genesis 2:24-25
My Lover and My Friend
Song of Solomon 2:1-16, 4:1-7, 4:15, 5:2-7, 5:16

I Love You More Than I Can Say
John 3:16
I Am Your Peace
Exodus 3:13-15
Never
Ecclesiastes 9:11, Matthew 10:22, Matthew 24:13
The Eagle
Isaiah 40:31
Wisdom
Proverbs 4:7
The First
Proverbs 18:22
The Lady in Waiting: Daddy's Little Girl
Proverbs 18:22
God's Leading Man
Psalms 84:11, Proverbs 18:22, Isaiah 53:2, Jeremiah 29:11

WORK CITED

Tyndale Life Application Study Bible. Wheaton, IL: Tyndale House Publishers, 2004.

63

Don't miss out!

Visit the website below and you can sign up to receive emails whenever Tracey D Hill publishes a new book. There's no charge and no obligation.

https://books2read.com/r/B-A-THQPB-CIRTD

Connecting independent readers to independent writers.